The Official Icky Poo Book

by the
Editors
of Klutz Press

Klutz Press • Palo Alto, CA

Grateful Acknowledgements

Scott Stillinger

Mike Sherman

the Klutzniks, one and all

Design by MaryEllen Podgorski
and Betty Lowman

Illustrations by Ed Taber

Production by Elizabeth Buchanan

Icky Poo is a trademark of Klutz Press. The Icky Poo material is used under license from Applied Elastomerics, Inc. and is fully protected under United States patents 4,369,284 and 4,618,213.

Published by Klutz Press, Palo Alto, California.

Manufactured in the United States of America

ISBN 0-932592-90-2

4 1 5 8 5 7 0 8 8 8

Additional Copies:

Additional copies of this book may be ordered directly from the publisher. The last page has details, but please check with your local bookseller as well.

The Icky Poo Story

I t all started in John Chen's back yard laboratory. It
was fall, 1976, and Mr. Chen, a research physicist,
was doodling around with some odd materials known
as "gels." He'd been banished from the kitchen, but
with the help of a lawn sprinkler and some salvaged lab
equipment, he'd been able to re-establish his research
facility in the back yard where, unbeknownst to him
or his neighbors, the frontiers of Weird Science were
about to be pushed forward in a quantum leap.

Gels are odd mutts in a world of solids, liquids and gases, and they have never attracted enormous research interest—which helps to account for the spartan laboratory conditions Mr. Chen was working with.

As he poked around at his latest effort, an extremely gluey concoction that clung devotedly to the bottom of a dish, his first thoughts were those of failure; the stuff looked like it was going to be a mess to clean up. Indeed, it took a half-hour of effort and no less than 3 rolls of paper towels before Mr. Chen was able to extract the blob and throw it disgustedly into the trash.

It might have been the end. If Icky Poo is ever made into a movie, this moment will have to represent its darkest hour.

For a full day, the world's one and only sample of Icky Poo rested in Mr. Chen's trash basket, waiting for its short ride into oblivion. But the next day, as Mr. Chen was emptying the trash, he happened to notice something interesting: The "Blob" had taken an imprint of the inside of the dish—right down to the scratches. This was interesting enough to warrant a little further investigation. The rest of the trash went into the garbage. The "Blob" was saved and taken back inside.

Clearly, the material was "hard set," i.e., it had memory. Despite yesterday's extraction ordeal, it had managed to "remember" its shape. That was curious enough, but nothing compared to the next discovery, the one upon which it would one day stake its claim to the title "Most Disgustingly Appealing Substance in the World."

The "Blob" it turned out, was true Weirdness itself. It was a "clean glue"; it stuck, but left no residue.

From a materials science point of view, this was academically interesting. But from any more normal point of view, it was incredible.

Mr. Chen cut off a sample and gave it to his nephew, just to see what the effect would be on the adolescent mind. Predictably, there was an instant bond.

It wasn't long before Mr. Chen had brewed up a couple hundred gluey blobs with the idea of doing a little "street market survey." This was Silicon Valley, and entrepreneurialism was the local custom. He and his wife loaded their car up and set out for Fisherman's Wharf in nearby San Francisco. Armed with two boxes of their sticky blobs, and a folding card table, they were intent on setting up the world's first gluey blob lemonade stand.

They didn't wait long for their survey results. The boxes were empty in minutes as their lemonade stand became the center of a small, gluey induced riot. The last couple of samples were fought over by people waving fistfuls of money. Mr. Chen and his wife returned home, visions of an elastic gel empire dancing in their heads.

Within a few weeks, a local toy store was approached and soon became the world's one and only "Gluey Blob" outlet. Sales were impossible to keep up with, and, after a while, Mr. Chen stopped even trying. The second (and far more boring) chapter of the story was about to begin. It was time to secure a patent.

As many would-be inventors have discovered to their dismay, filing for a patent is many things, but primarily expensive, time consuming and no fun. Waiting periods of two and sometimes three years are not uncommon. For Mr. Chen the waiting period was made particularly long by virtue of the fact that a Japanese toy firm decided to help itself to the idea while the patent was still pending.

After having obtained a sample, the toy firm corresponded briefly with Mr. Chen about the product and various shapes it might be molded into, including an octopus shape. Abruptly, the correspondence was dropped and shortly thereafter, an octopus-shaped copy of the sample appeared on the Japanese market.

In the fall of 1982, an East Coast importer got a hold of the Japanese "Wall-Walker" product and the Christmas of that year saw one of the most frenzied fads of our era as millions of them were sold here in the U.S.

By 1983 (finally!) the patent was issued and Mr. Chen was in a position to reclaim the rights to his own invention. He refined and improved the formula (the Japanese never did get it right) and licensed a few manufacturers to sell the improved version. AT&T used the stuff to prevent light leakage from around optical fibers.

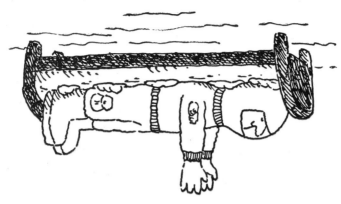

At the same time, Mr. Chen had some high tech hopes for the material. On the shuttle, he theorized that it would make a peerless glue to hold objects (like sleeping astronauts) in place in weightless space. On the outside of the shuttle, he envisioned its use as a micro-meteorite trap. A thick layer of the material could stop tiny meteorites ("high speed space dust") without damage. The trap could then be removed and the meteorites analyzed back on earth.

But meanwhile, back on earth, some basic research still remained. No one had ever really fully explored all the product's many dimensions. Most people became stuck on their first impression (sic). They couldn't get over that initial disgusting touch.

But to the inquiring mind willing to go a little deeper, there is a lot more to do with this amazing stuff than just hold it and scream.

From the moment when Mr. Chen walked into our offices and plopped a sample onto our ceiling fan, we knew what we had to do: Go where no other had gone before. With the sometimes barely controllable help of our local grammar school, we re-named the material "Icky Poo" and then devised 33 activities, each of which relies on the unique properties of John Chen's "elasto-meric gelatinous compound."

—The Editors of Klutz Press

The Care and Feeding of Icky Poo

Icky Poo is a mature substance that asks very little of its owner. It needs no batteries, it requires no special handling, there are no moving parts; it's almost completely care-free.

Notice I said "almost."

Where Can I Stick It?

Icky Poo does have a weakness, a "problem area," almost an obsession—latex paint.

8

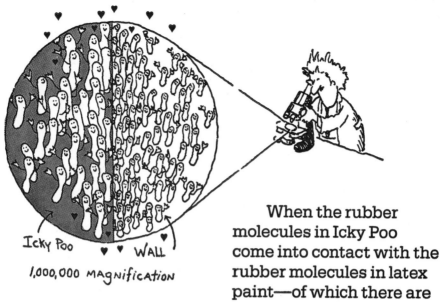

Icky Poo ♥ ♥ WALL

1,000,000 MAGNIFICATION

When the rubber molecules in Icky Poo come into contact with the rubber molecules in latex paint—of which there are many—there is an instant, deep, chemical bond, most clearly evidenced by a parentally-disapproved faint grey "wet" mark left on any latex-painted wall that has been used for target practice.

You can test this unfortunate habit by locating a piece of latex-painted wall that no one will ever see or care about. Then whap your Icky Poo onto it. The attraction is immediate. Even if your Icky Poo is brand-new clean, there will be a tell-tale ring-around-the-collar when you pull it off. Clear evidence of rubber-to-rubber affection.

This wouldn't be a problem except for the fact that latex paint is the basic flat wall paint, used almost

9

everywhere on interior walls (except, usually, for the kitchen and bathrooms). As a result, there is the potential for domestic problems.

Where does all this leave you and your insatiable need to stick your Icky Poo onto things? It just means you have to be a little careful in your choice of stickable surfaces. The primary rule: stay away from basic, flat, painted walls. Instead, stick with the world of non-latex-painted surfaces: Doors, furniture, floors, appliances, windows, glossy walls (kitchen, bathrooms), metal, tile, wood, plastic...etc. Paper (i.e., wallpaper) can also be a problem area, acting like a blotter and pulling out the oil in Icky Poo. But if you move quickly, and don't let your Icky Poo stay on the paper for any length of time, you should be OK.

One other prime rule: As we say around here, dirty Icky Poo is bad Icky Poo. It won't stick and it leaves dirt wherever it goes. As soon as yours starts to pick up a lot of dirt, lint, etc., take it in for a good washing with soap and water. Once it dries, it'll soon get back to its sticky self.

Can I Tear It?

In a word, yes. If you pull hard enough, Icky Poo will stretch to about 12 times its length... and then, in a heartbreaking moment, it will break. Also, if you ignore these warnings and persist in pulling it out to its maximum stretch, it will begin to show cracks and little tears, Icky Poo age wrinkles. The lesson is: Be kind to your Icky Poo, don't stretch it to its limit frequently, and it will last a lot longer.

Miscellaneous Concerns

Sorry, but Icky Poo is not for eating, nor cooking. It is a non-toxic substance but still, don't make a sandwich out of it. In the same cautionary vein, don't use it to sling heavy or pointed objects around.

Glossary

There are a few activities that are unique to Icky Poo, and as such, they have their own vocabulary. Here they are, along with some instructive illustrations.

Zapping A natural Icky Poo activity, almost irresistible. One hand hangs on while the other pulls back and releases. The pose is similar to archery, but most people are reminded of a parallel activity, namely, zapping things with rubber bands. (An activity now known as "mini-zapping.") Incidentally, we usually double up the paddle rope before we zap anything.

Zinging This might be unique to Icky Poo. It's a means of extending Icky Poo to its full length by just whipping it back and forth. It works because of its incredible elasticity. Try it. It's much easier done than said.

Paper Fetch:

If you've ever seen one of those wonders of nature movies with lizards that catch flies on their tongues, you'll pick up this game much more quickly.

1 Lay five or six pieces of paper on the floor, in a circle with a diameter of, say, six or seven feet. (The bigger the circle, the harder the game.) Get a partner with a similar fascination with lizards.

Mild Version

2 Stand in the middle of your circle with your Icky Poo rope at the ready.

3 The object of the game is to collect all the sheets off the ground by snagging them with the rope. Note that you have to sling your rope. If you can dangle your rope over the paper and "fish" with it, you're too close. Back off. No fair turning around, moving or bending over (this makes the papers behind you pretty difficult to grab).

4 If you miss, you switch with your partner. If you get a paper, you keep your turn. When the last sheet goes, whoever ends up with the most wins.

Paper Fetch: Wild Version

This is competitive paper fetch with no holds barred played for blood. It's not for the faint of heart. You'll need two players, each of whom should be armed with an Icky Poo Paddle Rope.

1 Both players have to separate themselves by 12 to 15 feet. Then, they each have to set four or five sheets of paper directly in front of them in a small semi-circle. Right at their feet.

2 At the gun, both players begin lashing their ropes out and snagging the other player's sheets. (To lash a Paddle Rope out, all you do is hang on to one end and sling the other end out. Remember those frogs?) You can't move your feet, but when you do snag a sheet,

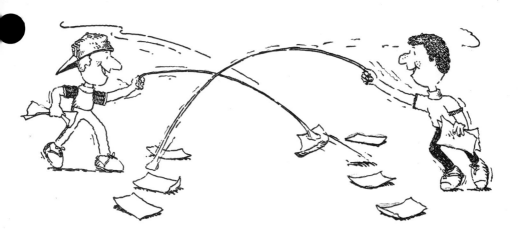

you have to put it down in front of you where it can, potentially, be grabbed back by the enemy.

3 If the ropes become hopelessly tangled, call an equipment time-out to separate them.

4 If your opponent snags one of your papers, and if you're quick enough, you can snag it back before he or she even gets it off the rope.

5 You can declare a winner by either of two ways. By playing against the clock, you can stop after 60 seconds to see who has the most sheets, or you can simply play until someone gets all the papers in front of them (not easy).

Frog Tongue

If you were a frog, this is the way you'd play darts.

1 Set up your dartboard on a safe surface like a window or refrigerator door. Put nine Post-It notes in a circle about the size of a dartboard. (Post-It notes are those little sticky squares of paper.)

Darts

2 About 5 feet in front of the board, install an imaginary "base line" beyond which you can't step. Flip a coin to see who goes first.

3 The object is to clean the Post-It notes off the surface by zapping them with your Icky Poo rope.

4 Take turns zapping off the Post-It notes. If you miss, you lose your turn. If you score, you keep it. Whoever has the most Post-It notes when the last one is zapped is the winner.

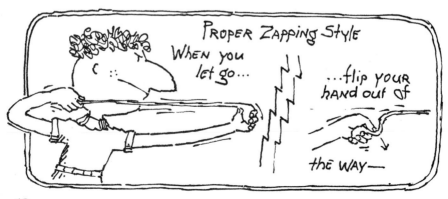

No Hands Catch

You may search the universe, but you will never find anything easier to catch than Icky Poo. All you have to do is get something in front of it. An arm, a leg, foot, nose...anything. The Icky Poo will do the catching. We play a points version of No Hands Catch that works for any number from two on up. It goes like this:

1 Wad up one of the Paddle Ropes into a lump. Make it as aerodynamic as you can.

2 Everybody spread out ten or fifteen feet and start tossing your Icky Poo around.

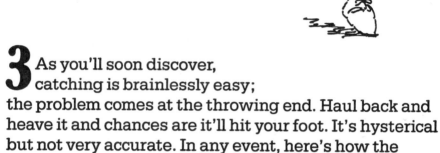

3 As you'll soon discover,
catching is brainlessly easy;
the problem comes at the throwing end. Haul back and
heave it and chances are it'll hit your foot. It's hysterical
but not very accurate. In any event, here's how the
scoring goes.

4 If the throw is so lame that no one could catch it
(happens all the time) that's 25 points taken from
the thrower's score. But if it is caught, the catcher gets
the points, as follows. If they can catch it on their foot,
that's 20 points; body, 10 points; forehead, 25 points;
hands, 0 points and, of course, nose, 50 points.

First one to 1 million points is the winner.

Quick

One of the first things you'll probably do with a new Paddle Rope is to hand one end to a friend and then, while talking soothingly to them, whap them with the other end by backing away and then letting go. Everyone does it. It's nothing to be ashamed of. The rope snaps back so fast that no one can possibly get out of its way. But, with one minor equipment change, you can level out the playing field and make an interesting game of it.

1 Get a medium balloon, inflate it, and tie one end to the Paddle Rope. The balloon acts as a parachute, slowing down the rope to something almost reasonable.

Draw

2 While your partner holds one end of the rope in front of his or her body, you should begin backing away with the balloon end. At some unannounced point, let go of the balloon and try to whap them. If they're able to block the balloon, switch places.

3 It's perfectly fair to try cheap psychological tricks in order to cause your partner to let down his guard. ("Look! Halley's Comet!")

Oscillation Jump Rope

This is a three person game. One to run, two to oscillate.

1 Locate your rope oscillators about 4 or 5 feet apart, each holding one end of the rope. (Rope oscillators are people who hold one end of the rope and wave it up and down. Simple job, fancy title).

2 It's your oscillators' job to set up a "standing wave" in the rope that's big enough for someone to run through. To do that, they have to get organized and wave their ends up and down together, in synch. Note that this is different from swinging a jump rope since the motion depends on the elasticity of the Icky Poo.

3 When the rope is going up and down high enough for the runner to fit through, they have to make a dash for it. If they can make it, they keep their spot. If they don't, if they get nailed by the rope, then they switch places with one of the holders.

Hold It

This is probably the basic Icky Poo game, and the one that takes the least practice. All you need to do is open the package to get the idea. Afterwards, there are a couple of subtle variations to it that are definitely worth trying.

(A) The Disgusting Handshake

A classic game with simple rules. Discreetly stick the Icky Poo to the palm of your hand and then work the crowd, pumping flesh. It's like shaking hands with a banana slug. Unforgettable.

and Scream

(B) The Shoe Thrill

The same basic idea as the Disgusting Handshake, just insert the Icky Poo into the toe of a shoe belonging to someone appropriate, and then observe from a safe distance.

INSERT HERE

Eeeeeek!

(C) "EEEEEEEEEEEEEEEK"

"Close your eyes, open your hand. Here's a chicken kidney I found."

Icky Concentration

A variation on the classic card game of Concentration. You'll need a deck of cards, a steel-trap of a memory, and Robin Hood's deadly eye.

1 Take your deck of cards and arrange them on the floor in a circle, a few feet wide. Locate yourself in the middle. Arm yourself with a paddle rope. Your opponent should do the same.

28

2 Somebody starts. Let's make it you. Zap any card you like. Pull it up, turn it over so that both of you can see it, then return it (by hand) to its place in the circle, face down. Burn its location and identity into your memory banks.

3 Your partner is next. He or she should do the same. At some point, one of you will turn over a card that matches a card that's already been turned over. When that happens, yell the following phrase: "HEY!"

If you yell first, you get to try to make the match by picking up the card's mate (This pickup can be done by hand, or by Icky Poo zap. Local rules vary.) If your partner yells first, he or she gets to try.

4 If somebody yells, but then can't find the mate (one chance only), then the turn passes and the other player gets a single chance. If both fail, then the card goes back to its place and you start over.

5 Cards that are successfully mated are put into the player's pile. When all the cards are claimed, the winner (naturally) has the larger pile.

Barn Door

This is not really a game so much as an exercise in hysterics. The rules are simple.

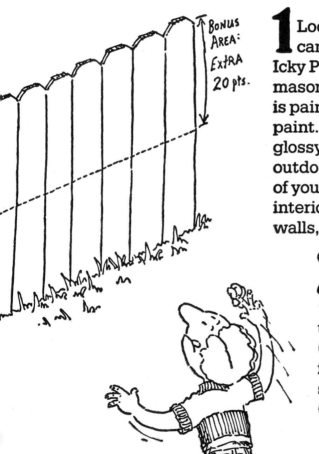

BONUS AREA: EXTRA 20 pts.

1 Locate a wall that you can safely pelt with Icky Poo. We have a masonry wall here that is painted with glossy paint. You might have a glossy kitchen wall, or an outdoor fence, or the side of your house...just avoid interior, latex-painted walls, or wallpaper.

2 Draw an imaginary line about 10 feet back and line up behind it. Put the (clean) paddle rope in your hand and squeeze it hard. (This is important.)

Now, relax your hand, haul back and try to hit it (the wall). The rules say you have to throw pretty hard.

3 ▶ If it leaves your hand, score 5 points.
▶ If it does not hit you in the foot, score another 5 points.
▶ If it hits the floor, score 10 points.
▶ If it hits the wall at all, score 15 points.
▶ If it hits the wall between eye-height and the ceiling, 20 extra points.

Scoring Examples:

You throw, it hits the ceiling. You get 5 points for getting it out of your hand, and 5 points for missing your foot. Total: 10 points.

You throw, it hits the floor. Again, a total of 10 points for getting it out of your hand and missing your foot—plus, a bonus of 10 points for hitting the floor. Total: 20 points.

You throw, it hits your foot. Five points for getting it out of your hand, but since you managed to miss both the floor and the wall, sorry, no more points.

Icky Poo Air Raid

Pretend you are a Lonely Island Nation living under the constant threat of paper airplane invasion. Your only defense is your Icky Poo anti-aircraft emplacement. This is your desperate situation. Here are the rules.

1 Locate yourself in front of a wall. This wall is your Motherland which you are attempting to defend. Opposing you, and standing at a distance of about 15 feet, is the enemy air force, consisting of your partner who is holding a well-made paper airplane(s).

2 At a signal, your partner launches his aircraft to-
ward your Motherland (wall). Your task is to shoot
it down by means of a well-aimed Icky Poo zap shot. If
you succeed, you switch places. Points are scored by
hits. First to 345,198 is the winner.

Icky Poo Tag

This is a sticky variation on the classic game of tag. You'll need to play it outdoors where you've got some running room.

1 Somebody has to be "it." Let's say that's you. Someone hands you the Icky Poo, and then takes off. Your job is to stick it back on them—or anyone else that's playing. Any means are fair—you can throw, lash, zap, sling it, anything that works—but you've got to make it stick. Just bouncing it off your victim doesn't count. (Remember, the cleaner the Icky Poo, the stickier it is. If it gets too dirty, you'll have to call an equipment time-out and head for the sink.)

SkyPoo

This game requires two extra pieces of equipment, namely, two paddle ball paddles. Paddle ball paddles are those wooden paddles that, when they're new, come attached by an elastic band to a little rubber ball. If yours are like ours, the little red rubber ball has long since come off. And that's fine, because for this game, you only need the paddle.

1 Take two paddles and one co-player. Head for the open spaces.

2 The object is a simple cooperative game of catch, but given Icky Poo's unpredictable flight pattern, the best way to play is to stand near one another and fling the Icky Poo high into the air. Straight up.

3 Then, your partner has to make the catch and send up his own Icky Poo pop-up. It sounds easy, but wait til you try it.

35

Refrigerator Relays

This is a chance to pit your Paddle Rope against someone else's in a contest of raw snail-like speed held on the door of your very own refrigerator.

1 You'll need two clean Paddle Ropes for this, each with an owner, or handler.

2 Both handlers should stand back a few feet from the chosen refrigerator and, on a signal, heave their Paddle Ropes onto its door. Both have to stick to the door at least as high as some agreed-upon mark.

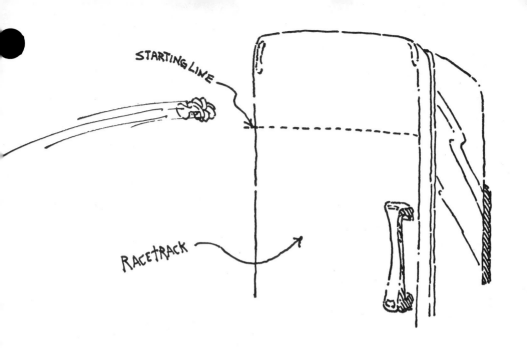

STARTING LINE

RACETRACK

(For example, in our kitchen, they have to hit at least as high as the scratch by the top hinge).

3 If one of the Paddle Ropes doesn't hit high enough, its owner has to retrieve it and try again (giving the other rope a significant head start).

4 Winner is the first to the floor.

Circle Zinging

A particularly good group game that solves the problem of how to spread one paddle rope around so that everyone gets a chance to play with it.

1 Any size group can play.
Minimum would be 4 or 5.

2 Draw a big circle on the ground, about 25 or 30 feet. Experiment to get the right dimension. In the center of the circle, draw an X.

3 Separate the group into teams of two. Let's make your team the first. Armed with your Icky Poo, step onto the "X" in the middle of the circle. Everyone else has to stay outside the circle. Your task, somehow, is to zing the paddle rope to your partner without stepping off the "X," and without allowing anyone else to intercept.

4 A little pre-arranged strategy can help a lot with this game, but you have to watch out for opponents standing behind you looking to grab your "backswing." Successful teams keep their turn, otherwise, they have to switch off.

Zig Zag

ou're going to need
2 paddle ropes for this
game, and a good-sized
crew, at least 8. The idea is to zing the paddle rope, in
a zig zag pattern, from one team member to the next.
"Zinging," in case you've forgotten, is described in the
introduction. It's a basic Icky Poo activity.

1 Pick your teams and line them up in two lines,
4 apiece, as in the illustration. Separate the lines
enough so that it takes full-intensity zinging to get
from one team member to the next.

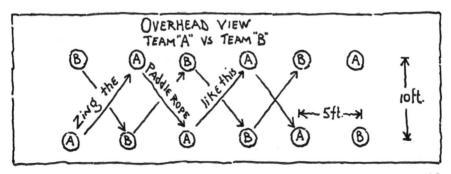

Zinging

2 Note that team members alternate in the lines so that the paddle ropes have to criss-cross back and forth. This criss-crossing gives rise to one of the best aspects to the game—interference.

3 If you can snag the other paddle rope with your own, then that counts as a broken-up zing and play stops while the two ropes are untangled (if necessary). When the ropes get untangled, they both go back to the players who were doing the zinging, not the grabbing, and it starts over.

4 First team to get their paddle rope down and back (one complete round trip) is declared the winner.

A successful snag

A Field Day with Icky Poo

I t has been our experience that two or three paddle ropes of Icky Poo can dominate a birthday party, regardless of how many other presents are available. As a result, we offer the following group games, designed to take advantage of Icky Poo's unique qualities.

To Finish Line

Hogtie Races

This is a variation on an old classic, burlap sack racing. The two main differences: You'll need three people per "hogtied group" and you can skip the burlap sacks.

Position your racers back-to-back-to-back. Absolutely no talking or laughing allowed. Wrap them up with your paddle rope. Keep the wraps between shoulders and knees and don't bother with any knots (a sticky rope needs no knots). At a signal, start your groups off. Keep extending the course as they go along. It's more fun that way.

Icky Squeeze

This was inspired by many unsuccessful barbed wire fence crossings. Stretch a paddle rope about six inches off the ground and attach the ends to something that won't move. (Or you can assign the job to a couple of idle bystanders who need something to do.) Stretch the second paddle rope above it—by about a foot or so. At a signal, racers have to run up to this sticky fence and squeeze between the two paddle ropes, cleanly, without touching. Any touching, and the "stickee" has to start over.

43

Balloon Roundup

A great birthday party game that requires a non-latex paint ceiling, at least two Icky Poo paddle ropes, and a collection of birthday party balloons.

1 If your balloons are helium, just let them float to the ceiling. If they're not, rub them against your hair to see if that will make them stick. If that doesn't work, use a little bit of tape for each one. Whichever way you go, the end result should be a ceiling populated with a bunch of balloons.

2 Every contestant must equip themselves with an Icky Poo rope. The idea is to de-populate the ceiling by zapping down the balloons with Icky Poo. The game begins at a signal and the winner (of course) collects the largest number. If you have more players than Paddle Ropes, you might set up a single elimination tournament, and pass around the ropes as need be.

Icky Picky Poo

This is a landbound version of that esteemed swimming pool game, Marco Polo. It's another great way for a group to play with a single paddle rope. You'll need at least 6 players and a wide open field with agreed-upon boundaries. How big a field depends on how many players.

1 Someone has to be "it." Once you've settled the occasionally tricky issue of who that's going to be, hand them a paddle rope and blindfold them with a bandana.

2 This game does not permit running. Only fast walking. All the other players scatter about. Whoever's "it" now hollers "Icky Picky" and everyone else has to holler back "POO." Based on these sound clues, the "it" player gives chase to the other players (only walking, don't forget).

3 As he's giving chase, he can swing his paddle rope around in an effort to snag someone. Other players can dodge or jump as much as they like. But if they get snagged, they have to join the "it" player by putting their hands on his/her hips, conga line style.

4 Now another round starts. The only difference is that the person second in line does not have to close their eyes and can holler directions to the paddle rope swinger.

5 As each player is snagged, they have to join the conga line until finally, only one person is left. When they are finally snagged, it's time for a new "it" person.

The No Game

This is a unique party game that relies on Icky Poo's extraordinary effect on people who are in close physical contact with it. Some people are very anxious to win the No Game, and others, just as anxious to lose it. And then, of course, there are a few who go back and forth. As you'll soon see, this is probably the best grown-up game in the book.

1 You'll need a group of people together...a classroom of kids, a dinner party of grown-ups, or almost anything in between.

48

2 The rules are very simple. Someone is selected to start. The Icky Poo is ceremoniously wrapped around their right hand (if they're right handed; left, if they're left-handed). Make sure the Icky Poo is at maximum Icky Poo-ness.

3 The only way the Icky Poo holder can get rid of their Icky Poo is to get someone else to say the word "no" in conversation. Plus, all conversations must begin with a hand-shaking. Note that it has to be the word "no." Synonyms, like "forget it," "you're out of your mind," "negative"...etc., are fine.

4 Reverse Variation: At some gatherings, both young and old, you will find those in attendance will love to have the Icky Poo clinging slimily to their hand. If you have one of those groups, and they are just about as common as their opposites, simply make one change in the rules: In order to *take* the Icky Poo from someone, you have to get *them* to say the word "no" in conversation.

Tactile

In John Chen's Icky Poo factory, a small fraction of the production is set aside every day for special treatment. In a separate final step, ball-shaped pieces of Icky Poo are permanently de-stickified, their "glue" is taken away and they become non-sticky gel balls. To most people, this seems like utter foolishness. Icky Poo without the "icky"? The mind recoils in horror. Why?

The reason turns out to have some real value. Hospitals and physical therapists purchase the balls because of their therapeutic value in hand and forearm exercises. They can be squeezed endlessly and their resilience is perfect. Plus, they have an extremely attractive quality to their "squeezability" that might be hard to explain, but is even harder to ignore.

Thrills

Those of us who don't have the "fixed" version of Icky Poo can still duplicate the effect very easily. Simply take an Icky Poo paddle rope and cover it in plastic Saran wrap. You can squeeze your covered Icky Poo for a cheap tactile thrill; take off your shoe and step on it for a solo foot rub; or just toss it around in a game that we call "Blob Ball" catch. Afterwards, the Saran wrap comes off easily, and your Icky Poo is returned to you.

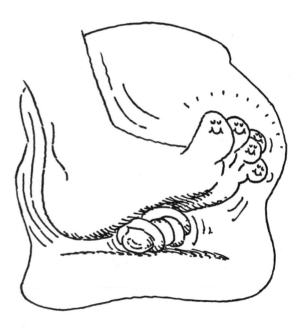

Grocery Bag

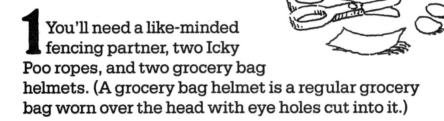

This is part-game, part-chaos with rules that are meant to be broken. The inspiration is fencing, but the fact that Icky Poo is not as rigid as most fencing foils demands a few modifications.

1 You'll need a like-minded fencing partner, two Icky Poo ropes, and two grocery bag helmets. (A grocery bag helmet is a regular grocery bag worn over the head with eye holes cut into it.)

2 At a signal, both combatants don their helmets, bow ceremoniously, and then begin to lash each other furiously with their Icky Poo ropes. You can dodge and run around as much as you like, but it's cheating to hang onto your helmet since the object is to pull it off with your Icky Poo.

Banzai

As soon as a successful "helmet removal" takes place, both combatants must stop lashing, bow to each other once again, and start over.

3 A full match is determined in a "best-of-three" contest.

Electric Icky

Whereas many of the games in this book rely on the paddle rope's phenomenal elasticity, this one depends on its disgustingness, which is why it's one of the most guaranteed winners here.

1 You'll need a group of at least 10. Your average birthday party should do fine.

2 Everybody sits down crosslegged in two lines, facing each other, a few feet apart. Eyes should be closed. Minds blank.

3 At the head of the lines sits a referee. He or she should be holding two paddle ropes all wadded up into two disgusting balls. Make sure the Icky Poo is clean so it sticks at maximum intensity.

4 All of the players should sit with their hands down on the ground at their sides, palms up. At some unannounced point, the referee will simultaneously place two balls of Icky Poo into the open palms of the players sitting directly next to him. They should be the first players in their respective lines.

5 As soon as he does that, the race is on. The object is to pass the Icky Poo down the line, hand to hand to hand. Eyes must stay closed, and the Icky Poo must touch every hand as it goes down the line. When a player receives the Icky Poo in his open palm (no moving of the hand until the Icky Poo is in it), he then passes it to his other hand and on to the next player.

6 When the last person in a line receives the Icky Poo, that line is finished. But before victory can be claimed, the last person must open their eyes and heave the Icky Poo across the way where it must stick to the chest of the player opposite them.

Icky Poo Plop

This is a cross between musical chairs and the myth of the Sword of Damocles (in which an inhospitable Greek king hung a sword by a thread over a chair at one of his banquets). Our version is a good bit more benign and makes an excellent birthday party game for kids, although there are definitely parts that appeal across many generation gaps.

1 You'll need a chair, a paddle rope, a 3x5 card, and some Scotch tape. Pull the chair into the middle of a room and step up on it with your card and tape. Ideally, you'll have a light fixture that you can tape the

card to (we did). Otherwise, fold the card in the middle, make an "L" of it, and tape it firmly to the ceiling.

2 Now, take your paddle rope and stick it to the 3x5 as shown. It should dangle down menacingly. Watch and see how long it takes to fall. If your Icky Poo is clean (and thus sticky) it will take anywhere from 10 seconds to 60 seconds, depending on how hard you stuck it (and other factors which we can't figure out).

5 SECONDS OR less MEANS you NEED to WASh youR Icky Poo—.

3 Once you've established that your paddle rope falls in a random, but reasonable period of time, you're ready.

4 Like most classics, the game is simple: Everybody has to take their chances on being in the chair when the Icky Poo finally plops. Pick a song that everybody knows, then pick a "volunteer" to start. They have to sit down, recite the first line of the song, and jump up to make room for the next player. (Set an order of players before you start.) The next player recites the next line, jumps up for the next player...

5 Sitters are not allowed to look up, of course, and when someone becomes a "ploppee," they are allowed to re-stick the paddle rope for the next go-round, then get in last in line.

57

Goalie Icky

A great, perhaps even the greatest, group game with Icky Poo. Works best with groups of about 8 to 14. You'll probably need a small outdoor area, or a play room that has been cleared of breakables and thoroughly approved for high energy games. The only extra equipment you'll need is a balloon.

1 Break your group up into two teams. Each team has to appoint someone as a goalie. The goalies have to arm themselves with a paddle rope and then plant themselves in the respective back corners of the playing area.

2 Once they've located themselves in their spots, the goalies should draw an imaginary "X" on the ground and cover it with a foot. Henceforward, that foot cannot move.

3 Everyone else gathers in the middle of the room and at a signal, tosses the balloon up. The object now is simple: bat the balloon across the playing area to your goalie who has to zap it with his Icky Poo, scoring a point. The key rule is no grabbing of the balloon, only batting.

4 That's it. The rest is a free-for-all. Short of outright mayhem, everything else goes. You can interfere, hold opponents, whatever works.

Team Toss

Another group game that gets better the larger your group. Minimum number would be about 8 players (with 4 paddle ropes); maximum would be millions.

1 You'll need two players per paddle rope. Line them up in two straight lines, parallel to one another. Each player should be able to reach across and touch his teammate.

2 Wad up your paddle ropes into their "aerodynamic mode." At a signal, players have to toss across to their partners. Partners have to catch with no hands allowed.

A successful catch means both partners back away from each other a single step. A drop means the partners have to retire from the field in disgrace.

3 The winning team, of course, is the last one left.

Lunch Table Poo

A two-player game designed for lunch tables and that period of time, after the trays have been cleared, but before the bell rings.

1 You can play with one or two paddle ropes. You'll also need some scraps of paper and a roll of Scotch tape, or, even better, a pad of sticky Post-It notes.

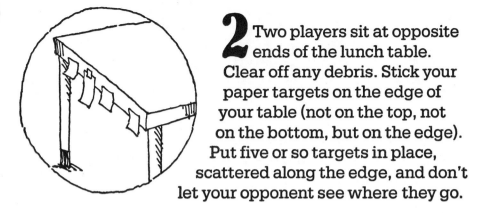

2 Two players sit at opposite ends of the lunch table. Clear off any debris. Stick your paper targets on the edge of your table (not on the top, not on the bottom, but on the edge). Put five or so targets in place, scattered along the edge, and don't let your opponent see where they go.

3 Meanwhile, he should be doing the same thing. Now you're ready.

4 The object of the game is to snag your opponent's targets off his edge of the table. You'll be shooting blind, since you shouldn't be able to see them, but, then, so will he.

5 The best way to snag is to zap your paddle rope, aiming a little over the edge. Do it right and it will wrap around the edge of the table and, if a target is there, snag it and bring it back.

6 Winner, of course, is the first to clean off all five.

Stickyball

This is two-person rainy day baseball. You'll need a plastic whiffle ball bat and a playroom that you can run around in.

1 Finding an approved playing room is often the trickiest part. A carport, garage or ping pong type of room would be perfect. Wash your Icky Poo well. It has to be max sticky.

2 Establish one base and home plate. Your base ought to be five or six good-sized steps from home.

The pitcher stands on the base and, by wadding up the Icky Poo and then holding it in a pinch, carefully tosses it to the batter.

3 The batter then takes a full-on swing. If he connects, the Icky Poo will stick to the bat (the first time this happens, it is very strange). The batter then drops the bat (with Icky Poo attached) and walks—fast—to the only base (no running indoors!). Meanwhile, the pitcher has to retrieve the bat, pull off the Icky Poo and tag the runner out before he gets back to home plate. We play that you can throw the Icky Poo if necessary, but you might want to amend that depending on house rules.

4 A successful "out" means that pitcher and batter switch. Strike-outs occur after 3 misses, and you have to swing at anything even remotely reasonable. Also, you can't stay on the base. You have to get back to home.

Flypaper Trashball

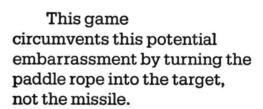

As you've undoubtedly long since discovered, Icky Poo is one of Nature's
most misguided missiles.
People have been known
to stand in front of a large
target pinned to a wall,
and from arm's length,
rear back, let fly, and miss
entirely. The wall.

This game
circumvents this potential
embarrassment by turning the
paddle rope into the target,
not the missile.

1 Find a place to hang the two paddle ropes down to about eye height. Keep them an inch or three apart. Here in our Icky Poo research facility we have used a ceiling fan and a light fixture. Don't stick it straight to the ceiling. It'll probably leave a mark, and won't stay long enough anyway.

2 Once the two paddle ropes are in place, you've got your target. Now the object is to just ball up some newspaper (or similar) and let fly. Baskets are scored when the paper sticks.

3 You can form teams or not. Set rules about how far back you have to be...etc. Let your imagination fly.

Co-Op Icky

When you pull your paddle rope out to its full extension, and then let go, it will come zinging back at better than 80 mph. This approaches major league fastball speed and explains why it is impossible to avoid Icky Poo when your "friend" has let go of his end when the two of you are playing tug of war.

However, there is a two-person cooperative way to play this game which is quite challenging mostly because it demands ESP-quality communication skills.

1 Find a partner who you can trust. A great deal.

2 Each of you begin stretching a paddle rope. For beginners, with poor communication skills, 10 feet separation is fine. For advanced, highly-communicative players, back up a good bit further.

3 The object of this cooperative game is to release both ends simultaneously so that the paddle rope collapses in the middle and falls harmlessly to earth. To have any chance of this, you have to talk to one another with great precision. ("Let go of your end on the count of three point two five five four...") As I mentioned before, you're dealing with high-speed Icky Poo here, so your reflexes better be highly tuned.

Spud

his is a classic group street game, modified to accommodate the particular qualities of our favorite elastic gel.

1 Get your group together, any number from three on up works. Find yourself some wide-open spaces.

2 Everyone has to stand clumped together, touching. Whoever's holding the Icky Poo suddenly throws it into the air—straight up—and then, while it's still airborne, hollers out someone's name.

3 The "named one" has to stay there and make the catch. Everyone else has to scatter. As soon as the catch is made, the catcher hollers "Spud!" Everyone else has to freeze.

4 The catcher now has to zing someone else, but they have to do it in 4 "zings" or less. Everyone else counts out loud…"S"…"P"…"U"…"D" as the paddle rope zings out and back. The target can dodge as much as they like without lifting one foot off the ground.

5 If the target gets zinged, they pick up a letter, "S," and the game starts over. If they don't get zinged, the catcher picks up a letter and the game starts over. When you get to "SPUD" you have to step out. Last one in is the winner.

Icky Icky Scrub Scrub

The next time you're in the tub, take your Icky Poo with you. Not only will you clean it up by getting it all wet and soapy, but you'll also discover a whole new dimension to irresistible sliminess. You'll be disgusted with yourself for loving it.

Lint Buster

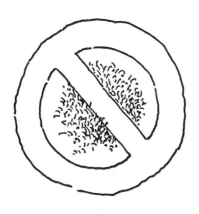

In the midst of all these less-than-serious activities, we thought a small note of raw utility wouldn't be completely out of place here at the end; and with that in mind, we include this final helpful hint.

At the risk of taking some of its fun quotient away, it must be said that Icky Poo is a world-class lint remover. John Chen sells blobs of it to the electronics industry where they use it to clean up the dust and lint on computer keyboards. This book, for example, was written on an Icky Poo-cleaned keyboard.

For those of you unburdened by any computers or keyboards, Icky Poo will do an amazing job on sweaters or woolens. As a lint buster, it has no living equal.

Mail Order Information

Icky Poo Paddle Ropes $4.00 each

For people interested in
building up a larger collection
of Icky Poo, these are extra
paddle ropes, identical to
what came with this book.

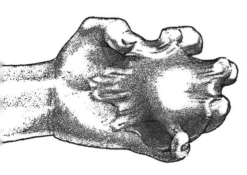

Glueballs® $5.50 each

John Chen's first toy idea is
available in the shape of two
hemispheres of his elastic gel
under the name Glueballs.
About the size of a tennis
ball, but cut in halves.

The Icky Poo Zoo

Just as we were getting our book ready for the printer, John Chen arrived breathlessly in our office with the very latest in Icky Poo fashion: The Giant Amazon Glueworm and The Giant Amazon GlueSlug. Both of them walked right into our hearts. They're Amazon big, they're done with loving attention to anatomical detail and they're very near the top of the Icky scale.

We knew we didn't have much time, so we rushed around, got the artwork together, and at the last minute, managed to get them both onto this page. We hope you will welcome them into your home or garden soon.

Giant Amazon Glueslug™ $5.00

Giant Amazon Glueworm™ $5.00

The Pair, Giant Amazon Glueslug™ and Giant Amazon Glueworm™ $9.00

Smartballs™ $6.00 each

If you would like to try Icky Poo without the Icky, balls of the same material that have been destickified are also available. Some people, who have personal problems with the gluey feel to Icky Poo, have been known to fall in love with the non-sticky form. A matter of personal choice.

Glueball, Giant Amazon Glueslug, Giant Amazon Glueworm, and Smartball are all registered trademarks of Applied Elastometrics, Inc.

Free Catalogue

We also publish a mail order cata-logue several times during the year which contains all of our titles, as well as a diverse variety of other things which we happen to like. If you would like a copy of The Flying Apparatus Catalogue, please just drop us a line, or call.

Klutz Mail Order
2121 Staunton Court ● Palo Alto, CA 94306
(415) 424-0739

Mail Order Blank

Quantity	Description	Price
	Add 10% for Postage	
	Total Enclosed (check or money order)	

Name _____

Street _____

City _____ State _____ Zip _____

Telephone (___) _____

IP   Klutz Enterprises●2121 Staunton Ct.●Palo Alto, CA 94306
(415) 424-0739

Order Icky Poo paddle ropes ($4.00), Glueballs ($5.50), Glueslugs ($5.00), Glueworms ($5.00), or Smartballs ($6.00) directly through the mail. Add 10% of your order total for shipping. Please use the form above and note that prices are guaranteed through the end of 1991. Afterwards, call for updates.